D1501761

SO YOU WANNA BE A DJ

MICHELLE GARCIA ANDERSEN

Rourke
Educational Media

rourkeeducationalmedia.com

Before Reading:

Building Academic Vocabulary and Background Knowledge

Before reading a book, it is important to tap into what your child or students already know about the topic. This will help them develop their vocabulary, increase their reading comprehension, and make connections across the curriculum.

1. *Look at the cover of the book. What will this book be about?*
2. *What do you already know about the topic?*
3. *Let's study the Table of Contents. What will you learn about in the book's chapters?*
4. *What would you like to learn about this topic? Do you think you might learn about it from this book? Why or why not?*
5. *Use a reading journal to write about your knowledge of this topic. Record what you already know about the topic and what you hope to learn about the topic.*
6. *Read the book.*
7. *In your reading journal, record what you learned about the topic and your response to the book.*
8. *After reading the book complete the activities below.*

Content Area Vocabulary
Read the list. What do these words mean?

alter
distinguishing
humble
manipulating
muffled
organized
personable
recognition
selective
varies

After Reading:

Comprehension and Extension Activity

After reading the book, work on the following questions with your child or students in order to check their level of reading comprehension and content mastery.

1. *What are the most important things a DJ needs to know? (Summarize)*
2. *Why does a DJ need to have good communication skills? (Infer)*
3. *Where can DJs find work? (Asking Questions)*
4. *What are your top three skills that would help you be a successful DJ? (Text to Self Connection)*
5. *What types of things can you do right away to prepare for a career as a DJ? (Asking Questions)*

Extension Activity

Research free DJ apps. With your parents' permission, download a few of them to play with. Which has the best features? Which needs improvement? Think about how you would design the perfect DJ app based on your experience with these apps. Then head over to the app lab at www.code.org and give it a shot. Maybe you could build the next great DJ app!

TABLE OF CONTENTS

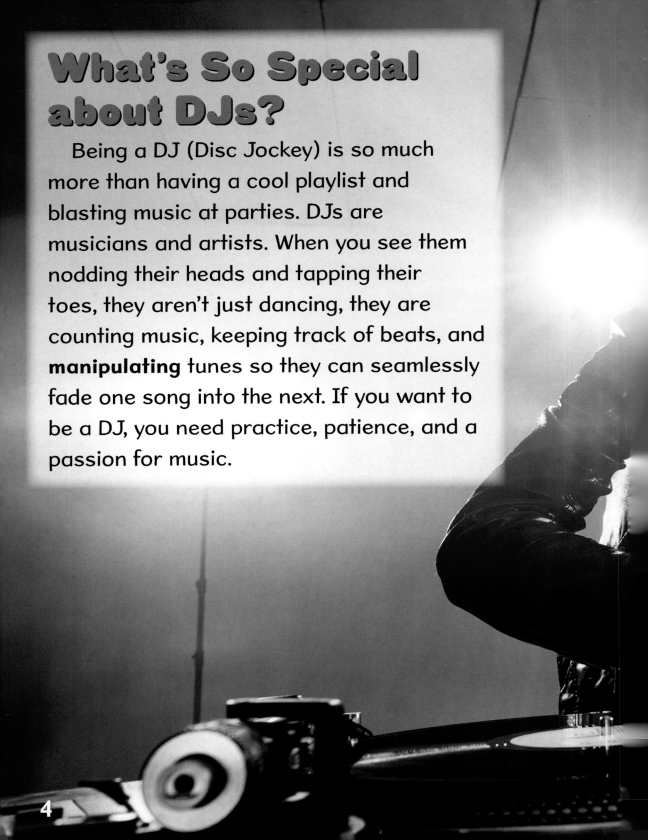

What's So Special about DJs?

Being a DJ (Disc Jockey) is so much more than having a cool playlist and blasting music at parties. DJs are musicians and artists. When you see them nodding their heads and tapping their toes, they aren't just dancing, they are counting music, keeping track of beats, and **manipulating** tunes so they can seamlessly fade one song into the next. If you want to be a DJ, you need practice, patience, and a passion for music.

DID YOU KNOW?!

In 1909, a 16-year-old named Ray Newby played records on the radio—and became the world's first DJ, decades before the term disc jockey was invented!

So how do you know if you have what it takes to become a DJ? First, you have to really love music. You will spend a lot of time listening to and collecting different types. Second, it helps to have an outgoing personality. The best DJs are the ones who interact with their audiences. Third, you have to be willing to work hard to stand out.

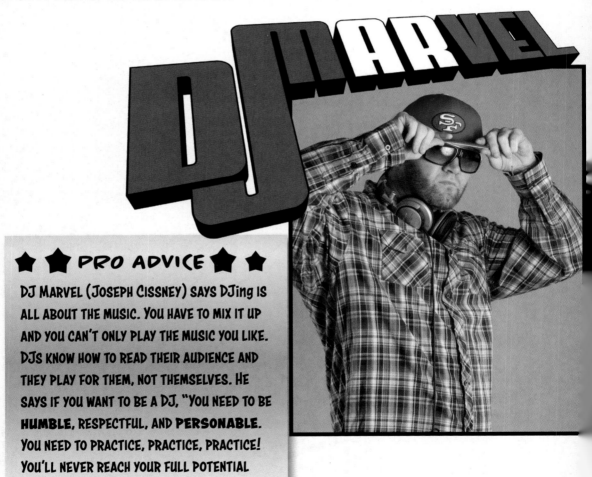

★ ★ PRO ADVICE ★ ★

DJ MARVEL (JOSEPH CISSNEY) SAYS DJing IS ALL ABOUT THE MUSIC. YOU HAVE TO MIX IT UP AND YOU CAN'T ONLY PLAY THE MUSIC YOU LIKE. DJS KNOW HOW TO READ THEIR AUDIENCE AND THEY PLAY FOR THEM, NOT THEMSELVES. HE SAYS IF YOU WANT TO BE A DJ, "YOU NEED TO BE **HUMBLE**, RESPECTFUL, AND **PERSONABLE**. YOU NEED TO PRACTICE, PRACTICE, PRACTICE! YOU'LL NEVER REACH YOUR FULL POTENTIAL UNLESS YOU ARE PRACTICING AND CHALLENGING YOURSELF."

DJs use the mic to get their audiences energized and excited.

DJ Skills

There are lots of software programs that can teach you how to become a DJ. Some software will do a lot of the work for you. However, many DJs will tell you that it is best to learn the craft before taking shortcuts. DJs know a lot of tricks, such as beatmatching, phrasing, equalizing, cutting, and scratching.

DJs used to lug their music with them to their gigs. It was a lot of work hauling records and CDs! Now their music is stored on computers.

Becoming a DJ is expensive. You'll need equipment and lots of music. Take your time and do your research before making any purchases.

Beatmatching is matching the tempo or speed of one song with another. A DJ will **alter** the speed or BPM (beats per minute) of one song with another so the two songs sound like one. You'll need a good ear and the ability to count music. When you first start DJing, you might want to have software beatmatch for you, but it's always a good idea to learn how to do this without the aid of technology.

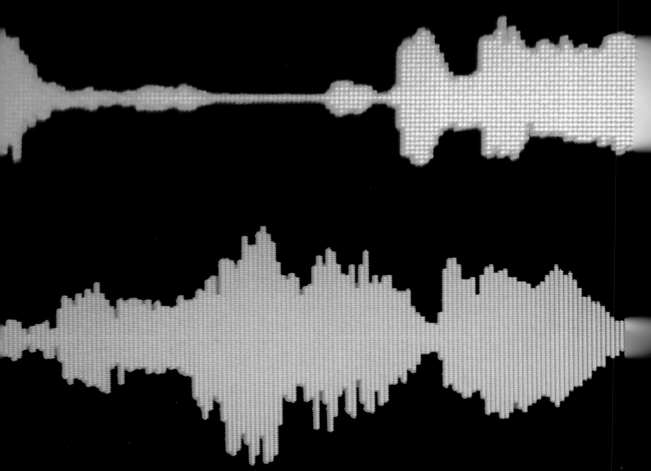

After you've matched your beats, you'll need to listen for the right moment or phrase to combine both tracks. This is called phrasing. If you don't combine your tracks with the right beat or phrase, your mix will sound clunky or off.

FAST FACT:
Beatmatching started in the 1960s.

Sometimes you might struggle to hear all the sounds in your mix. Sounds travel in waves at various speeds known as frequencies. The wave frequency determines the sound's pitch. Our ears have trouble **distinguishing** sounds that are perfectly matched in frequency. Either the sounds become very loud or they become **muffled**.

DJs use a device called an equalizer (EQ) to control this. An artful DJ knows when to turn certain sounds up or down.

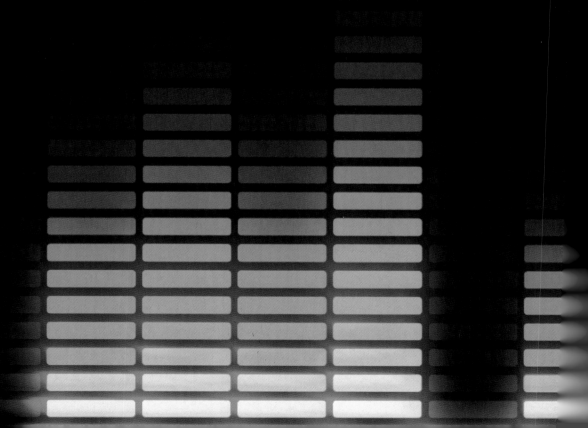

DID YOU KNOW?!

Radio commentator Walter Winchell (1897–1972) coined the term *disc jockey* in the 1930s.

Some DJs participate in competitions. On October 1, 2017, 12-year-old DJ Rena, from Japan, took first place at The DMC World DJ Championship—the world's largest DJ competition.

Cutting is another technique DJs often use. Cutting is switching instantly from one song to the next without beatmatching. It requires a crossfader and allows the DJ to bounce back and forth between turntables single-handedly.

DID YOU KNOW?!
You can find online and in-perso DJ lessons for kids. There are even DJ summer camps!

Some DJs or turntablists are known for scratching. Scratching is done by moving vinyl records back and forth on a turntable by hand and creating a totally new sound. The more you practice, the more tricks you'll learn and the better DJ you will become.

DJs use special needles and turntables meant for scratching. The needle remains in the same groove and does not scratch across the record.

Create Some Noise

Eventually, you'll want to record a mix. You'll need a DJ name—this will be your brand and how people will refer to you in the business. When you are ready, upload your mix online. Create a website or social media page so people can find you and you can start booking gigs.

Many DJs start out learning how to DJ in their bedrooms. In fact, this is so common, they have a term for it: 'Bedroom DJs.'

Go to the places you want to play and find ways to contribute. Are you willing to work for free or very little to build a following? Get to know the people you want to work with. Show them you are serious and willing to work hard.

Types of DJs

Think about what type of DJ you want to be and what type of music you want to play. Do you ever think about creating your own music? Then becoming a DJ/Producer might be for you.

A DJ needs to be tech-savvy. It's a good idea to shadow a professional to learn more about the industry.

FAST FACT:
There are five main types of DJs: club, mobile, producer, radio, and turntablist. Many DJs specialize in two or more types.

A DJ/Producer plays other people's music while also mixing in sets of their own music. Being a DJ/Producer is a faster way to gain **recognition** with fans and will likely book you more gigs. People will come to see you perform as well as hear your mix.

DiD YOU KNOW?!
DJ Calvin Harris made $48.5 million in 2017, according to *Forbes* magazine.

Perhaps you've thought about becoming a radio DJ. The job of a radio DJ **varies** from station to station. You might be responsible for announcing the weather, sports, and news, in addition to playing music. You might have a lot of freedom in what you play or you might be restricted to certain songs or artists.

If you want to become a radio DJ, you need to be willing to work all hours of the day. Radio stations play all day, every day.

FAST FACT:
The median annual earnings for radio announcers was $31,400 in 2016, according to the U.S. Bureau of Labor Statistics.

Many radio DJs have college degrees. They often go to school and major in broadcast journalism or communications. They also often start their careers as interns or part-time radio station employees, working in promotions, marketing, or other areas before they get their chance to go on-air.

Some colleges and universities have their own radio stations. They play music, cover school athletics, and report news. If you're looking for a career as a radio DJ, starting as a student can give you experience and introduce you to others in the field.

DJ GEMINEYE BEGAN HIS CAREER DJING CLUBS AND BECAME KNOWN FOR HIS MIXES. WHEN ASKED TO GO ON-AIR AS A RADIO DJ, HE HAD TO LEARN TO OVERCOME HIS SHYNESS—HE IMAGINED HIMSELF TALKING TO A FRIEND. HIS LIGHTHEARTED CONVERSATIONAL STYLE MADE HIM AN INSTANT FAVORITE AMONG HIS LISTENERS. HE LEARNED THAT BEING HIMSELF AND BEING WILLING TO TRY NEW THINGS COULD OPEN DOORS FOR HIM.

DJ GEMINEYE IS NOW THE OFFICIAL DJ FOR THE UNIVERSITY OF OREGON'S FOOTBALL AND BASKETBALL TEAMS AS WELL AS TRACKTOWN USA. HE SAYS HE DOESN'T CARE IF HE'S PLAYING FOR A CROWD OF 50,000 PEOPLE OR A MIDDLE SCHOOL VALENTINE'S DANCE, AS LONG AS HE'S BEHIND THE TURNTABLES HE IS HAVING FUN. DJ GEMINEYE SAYS IF YOU WANT TO BE A DJ, "YOU NEED TO WORK REALLY HARD AND BE YOURSELF."

If you want to have more control over your schedule, you may want to be a wedding or event DJ. These mobile DJs can be more **selective** with their time. You'll need to be willing to take song requests from your audience. You'll also need to be comfortable speaking to a crowd.

Mobile DJs provide music for weddings, business parties, school dances, and other private events.

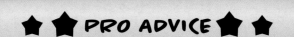

★ ★ PRO ADVICE ★ ★

DJ Hope is the owner of Pure Sound Entertainment. She's been DJing weddings for several years. She said one of the most challenging parts of being a wedding DJ is scheduling things far into the future. Most of her weekends are planned a year in advance. She said, if you want to be a wedding DJ, "You need to be incredibly ORGANIZED. Be willing to work really hard and put yourself out there."

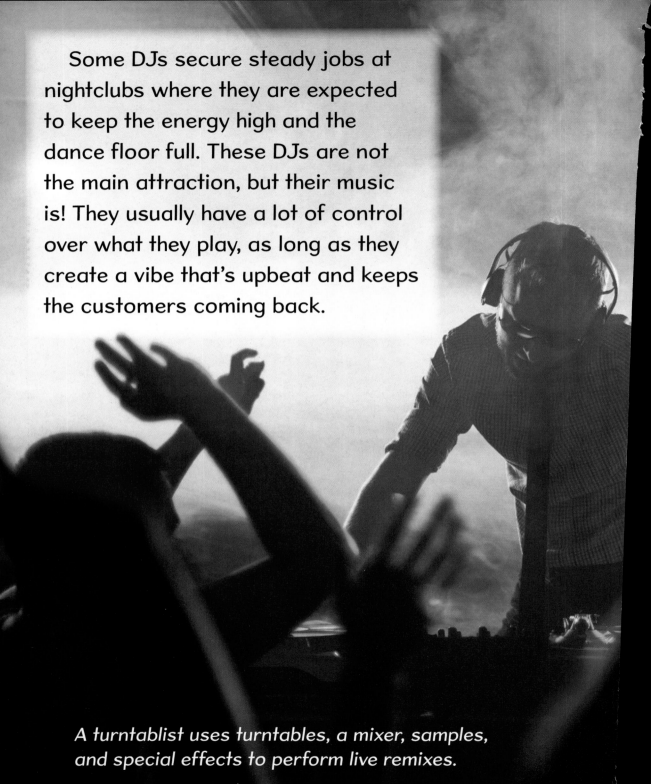

Some DJs secure steady jobs at nightclubs where they are expected to keep the energy high and the dance floor full. These DJs are not the main attraction, but their music is! They usually have a lot of control over what they play, as long as they create a vibe that's upbeat and keeps the customers coming back.

A turntablist uses turntables, a mixer, samples, and special effects to perform live remixes.

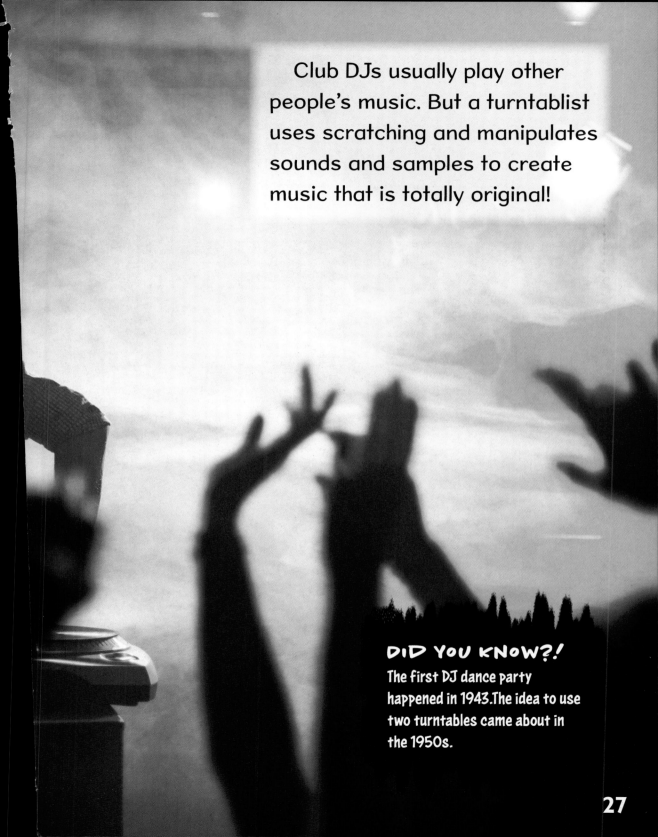

Club DJs usually play other people's music. But a turntablist uses scratching and manipulates sounds and samples to create music that is totally original!

DID YOU KNOW?!

The first DJ dance party happened in 1943. The idea to use two turntables came about in the 1950s.

It takes a lot of work to become a skilled DJ and success doesn't happen overnight. A good DJ knows how to read their audience. They know when to speed things up and slow things down. Whether it's on the radio, at a wedding, or at a club, there's a mix for every occasion and it's the DJ's job to create it.

Headphones are one of the most important pieces of DJ equipment. When you see a DJ wearing only one headphone they are usually listening to the crowd with one ear, and the track they want to mix with the other.

DID YOU KNOW?!
January 20 is National Disc
Jockey Day.

It's important to find ways to relax after DJing an event.
The constant energy and party atmosphere can take a while
to come down from.

Glossary

alter (AWL-tur): to make a change

distinguishing (diss-TING-gwish-ing): telling the difference between things

humble (HUHM-buhl): not boastful or proud

manipulating (muh-NIP-yuh-late-ing): to operate or move in a skillful way

muffled (MUHF-uhld): made a sound dull or difficult to hear

organized (OR-guh-nized): planned or scheduled with care

personable (PUR-suhn-uh-buhl): pleasant and likable

recognition (rek-uhg-NI-shuhn): to see or hear someone and know who the person is

selective (si-LEK-tiv): to choose carefully

varies (VAIR-eez): changes

Index

Show What You Know

1. What is beatmatching?

2. What does an EQ do?

3. What is scratching?

4. Name some of the skills needed to become a wedding DJ.

5. Name three important characteristics of a DJ.

Further Reading

Long, Hayley, *Vinyl Demand*, Accent Press, 2016.

Marlowe, Christie, *DJ*, Mason Crest, 2014.

Earl, C.F., *Hip Hop: A Short History (Superstars of Hip Hop)*, Mason Crest, 2014.

About the Author

Michelle Garcia Andersen lives with her husband and three kids in a music-filled home. Michelle loves all types of music, from classic rock and roll to country and everything in between. If Michelle were a DJ, she would be a wedding DJ.

Meet The Author!
www.meetREMauthors.com

© 2019 Rourke Educational Media

All rights reserved. No part of this book may be reproduced or utilized in any form or by any means, electronic or mechanical including photocopying, recording, or by any information storage and retrieval system without permission in writing from the publisher.

www.rourkeeducationalmedia.com

PHOTO CREDITS: Cover: ©maxoidos; p. 3: ©Nataly-Nete; p. 4: ©Daxiao Productions; p. 7: ©LightField Studios; p. 8: ©hurricanehank; p. 9: ©SIphotography; p. 10: ©edwardolive; p. 12: ©raspirator; p. 13: ©Wiki; p. 14: ©hurricanehank; p. 15: ©Daxiao Productions; p. 17: ©IBushuev; p. 18: ©MBI/©Alamy Stock Photo; p. 19: ©KatarzynaBialasiewicz; p. 20: ©Dmitri Ma; p. 21: ©wavebreakmedia; p. 22: ©TwilightShow; p. 24: ©Brian McEntire; p. 25: ©tirc83; p. 26: ©shironosov; p. 28: ©zhudifeng; p. 29: ©LuckyImages.

Edited by: Keli Sipperley
Cover and Interior design by: Rhea Magaro-Wallace

Library of Congress PCN Data

A DJ / Michelle Garcia Andersen
 (So You Wanna Be)
  ISBN 978-1-64156-472-4 (hard cover)
  ISBN 978-1-64156-598-1 (soft cover)
  ISBN 978-1-64156-713-8 (e-Book)
Library of Congress Control Number: 2018930508

Rourke Educational Media
Printed in the United States of America,
North Mankato, Minnesota